Snake & Lizard

**ROD THEODOROU
AND
CAROLE TELFORD**

First published in Great Britain by Heinemann Library
Halley Court, Jordan Hill, Oxford OX2 8EJ
a division of Reed Educational & Professional Publishing Ltd

MELBOURNE AUCKLAND
FLORENCE PRAGUE MADRID ATHENS
SINGAPORE TOKYO CHICAGO SAO PAULO
PORTSMOUTH NH MEXICO
IBADAN GABORONE JOHANNESBURG
KAMPALA NAIROBI

Designed by Susan Clarke
Cover design by Simon Balley
Illustrations by Adam Abel
Printed in Great Britain by Bath Press Colourbooks, Glasgow

00 99 98 97 96
10 9 8 7 6 5 4 3 2 1

ISBN 0 431 06368 0

British Library Cataloguing in Publication Data
Theodorou, Rod
   Snake & lizard. – (Spot the difference)
   1. Snakes – Juvenile literature 2. Lizards – Juvenile literature
   1. Title 11. Telford, Carole
   597.9'6

Acknowledgements
The Publishers would like to thank the following for permission to reproduce photographs:
Daniel Heuclin/NHPA p4; M. Krishnan/Ardea London Ltd. p5; Bob Gibbons/Ardea London
Ltd. p6; Richard Matthews/Planet Earth Pictures p7 *top*; Gary Bell/Planet Earth Pictures p7
bottom; Jen and Des Bartlett/Oxford Scientific Films p8; Tom McHugh/Oxford Scientific Films
pp9, 17 *top*; Michael Fogden/Oxford Scientific Films pp10, 11 *bottom*; Myer Bernstein/Planet
Earth Pictures p11 *top*; A.N.T./NHPA p12 *top*; J.P. Ferrero/Ardea London Ltd. p12 *bottom*;
Anthony Bannister/Oxford Scientific Films pp13, 17 *bottom*; Michael Leach/Oxford Scientific
Films p14; Karl Switak/NHPA p15; Peter Parks/Oxford Scientific Films pp3 *top*, 16; Babs and
Bert Wells/Oxford Scientific Films p18 *top*; Hans and Judy Beste/Ardea London Ltd p18
bottom; John Lythgoe/Planet Earth Pictures p19 *top*; Carol Farnett/Planet Earth Pictures p19
bottom; E.R. Degginger/Oxford Scientific Films p20; Breck Kent/Oxford Scientific Films p21;
Ron and Valerie Taylor/Ardea London Ltd p22; Ajay Desai/Oxford Scientific Films p23

Cover photographs reproduced with permission of Zig Leszczynski/Oxford Scientific Films
top; Karl Switak/Oxford Scientific Films *bottom*

Contents

Introduction

Lizards are **reptiles**. They are **cold-blooded**. This means they have to warm themselves up by lying in the sun each day. Most of them have **scaly** skin, a long, thin body and a long tail. There are over 3700 **species** of lizard. Most lizards are small. Geckos are some of the smallest; they measure less than the length of your hand. The Komodo Dragon is the largest, it can grow as long as a car.

A tiny Madagascar chameleon

A lizard has a light skeleton. This helps it to run fast.

Snakes are cold-blooded reptiles, too. They have long, thin bodies and no legs. Like lizards, they are covered in scales. There are 2400 species of snake. The largest of these is the reticulated python, which can grow up to 10 metres long.

A reticulated python

Humans have twelve pairs of ribs. Snakes have hundreds!

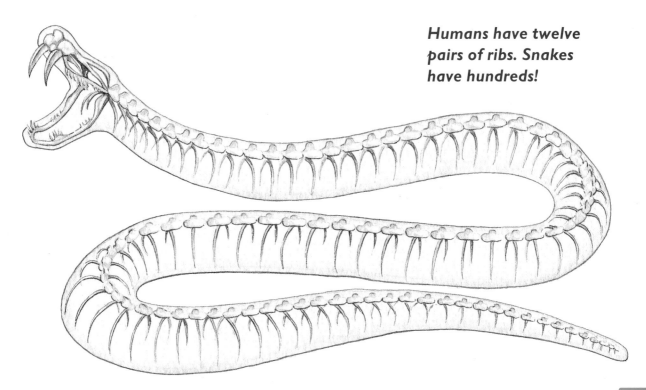

Where they live

Lizards live all over the world, mostly in hot places. They live on the ground and in trees. Lizards that live in places that are not very hot have to spend a lot of time sunbathing on rocks and walls, soaking up the sun. Lizards who live in hot places do not have to spend as long in the sun, but they have other problems. They have to hunt at night, when it is cooler.

The marine iguana is unusual because it lives by the sea.

The giant anaconda lives in rivers in South America.

Snakes live in every part of the world, too. Most snakes live in hot places. Most of them live on the ground. Some live in rainforests. Some snakes burrow into the sand to escape the heat of the sun, coming out in the cooler evening to hunt. Some burrowing snakes live underground all the time. In cooler places snakes, like lizards, have to sunbathe almost all the time. Some of them even **hibernate** in winter.

The tail and part of the body of a sea snake are slightly flattened, and act like an oar in the water.

Senses

Lizards have very good eyesight. Chameleons can move their eyes in different directions when looking for insects. When one eye spots an insect the other looks in the same direction so the chameleon can grab it.

Lizards can 'taste' the air in the same way that we smell things. They flick out their tongues to sense what is going on around them.

Geckos' eyes have special pupils that close up to keep out the glare of the daytime sun.

A pit viper snake can sense its prey in total darkness.

heat-sensing pits

Snakes have no **eardrums**, so they cannot hear noises. They 'hear' by sensing **vibrations** through the ground, and by flicking out their tongues, just like lizards.

Some types of snake, called pit vipers, have pits (holes) on their heads which help them pick up changes in the temperature around them. As living things give off heat, this helps them to detect other creatures nearby.

It's amazing!

Snakes do not have eyelids, as lizards do. Instead, snakes have a clear scale, called a spectacle that covers the eye. Snakes never blink!

Staying hidden

Many lizards need to be able to stay hidden, either to avoid their enemies or stalk their **prey**. Some have the same colour as the sand they live on. Some are the same colour as the leaves or bark of the trees they live in.

It's amazing!
Chameleons can change colour to stay hidden no matter where they are.

Snakes are often the same colour as their surroundings, too. Sometimes they are patterned to look like sand, gravel or leaves. Vine snakes have long thin bodies and hang from trees, swaying just like **vines** do. They are almost impossible to spot!

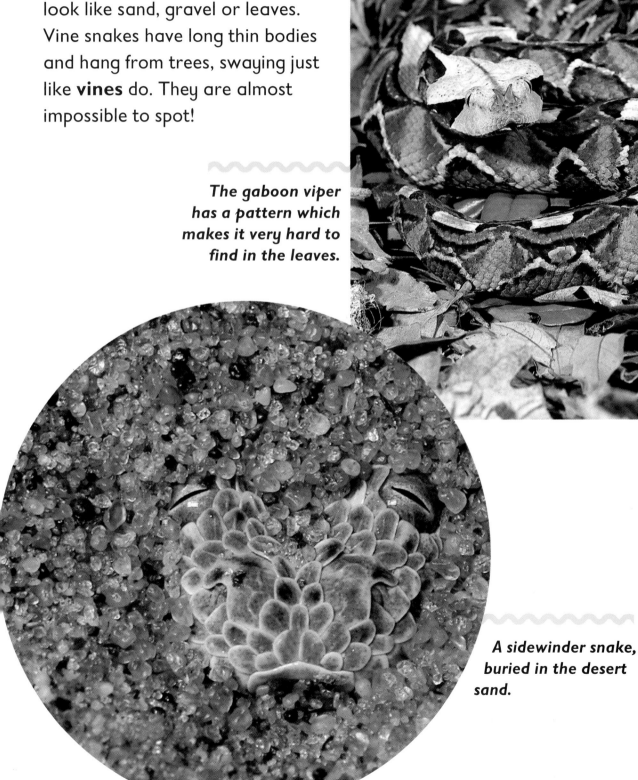

The gaboon viper has a pattern which makes it very hard to find in the leaves.

A sidewinder snake, buried in the desert sand.

Moving

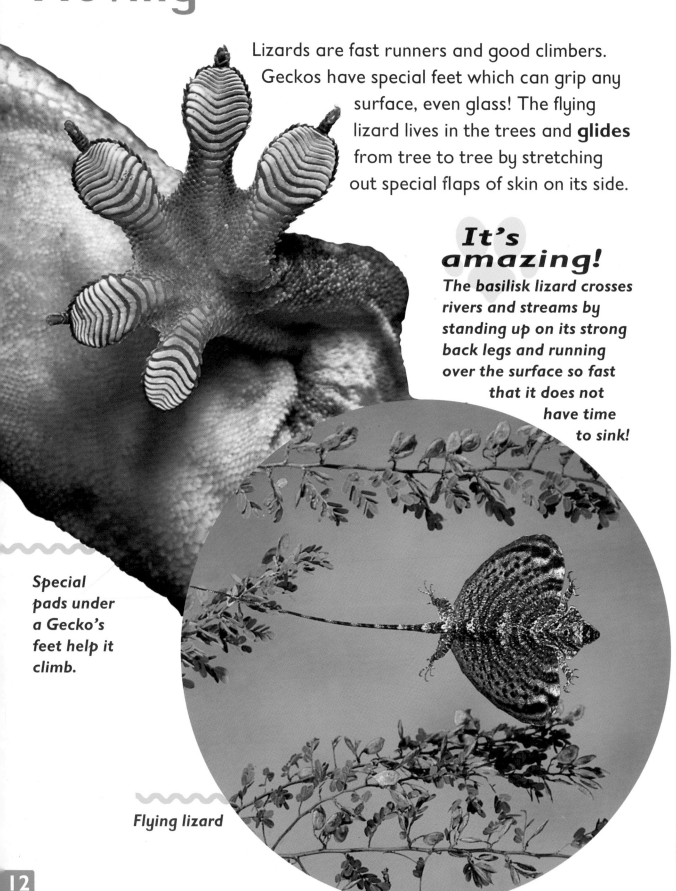

Lizards are fast runners and good climbers. Geckos have special feet which can grip any surface, even glass! The flying lizard lives in the trees and **glides** from tree to tree by stretching out special flaps of skin on its side.

It's amazing!

The basilisk lizard crosses rivers and streams by standing up on its strong back legs and running over the surface so fast that it does not have time to sink!

Special pads under a Gecko's feet help it climb.

Flying lizard

Many snakes move from side to side in 's' shapes. This pushes them along the ground and up trees. Big snakes find it tiring to move like this. They ripple the muscles along their spines and 'walk' on their hundreds of ribs. Tree snakes 'parachute' down from trees by stretching out their ribcage.

The sidewinder snake moves sideways over the desert sand.

Feeding

Lizards eat mostly insects. Some lizards, like the green iguana, eat different food as they grow up. They eat plants and insects when young, but eat nothing but plants when they are adults. Other lizards eat only one type of food. The marine iguana eats seaweed, which it dives into the water to collect.

The chameleon flicks out its incredibly long tongue to trap insects to eat.

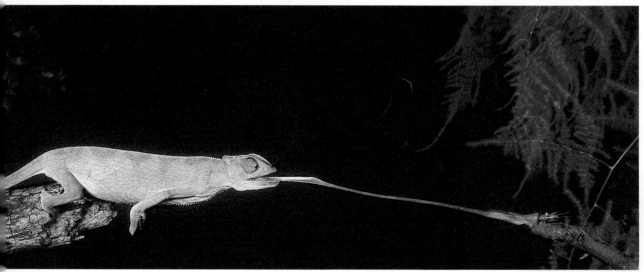

Egg-eating snake

All snakes are meat eaters. They cannot chew, so they have to swallow their food whole. They have a very loose-hinged jaw to help them do this, so they can open their mouths extra wide to eat large animals. The African egg-eating snake can swallow an egg that is bigger than its head. It also has special bones in its throat to crack the eggshell as it eats.

It's amazing!

A python may take over an hour to swallow a small deer!

Hunting

Lizards that hunt insects sneak up on their prey and then pounce and bite them. Some lizards, like geckos, are nocturnal – they only come out at night. They have especially good eyesight, to be able to catch insects in the dark.

A gecko eating a moth.

All snakes have sharp teeth. Some of them also have fangs which can inject a poison called venom into their prey. Other snakes kill their prey by constriction. They coil their bodies around the victim like a lasoo. Then they squeeze until the victim can no longer breathe and dies.

The fangs of a poisonous red-diamond rattlesnake.

It's amazing!

The spitting cobra squirts venom into its victim's eyes, to blind it so it cannot escape.

Defence

The blue-tongued lizard sticks out its bright blue tongue to scare off enemies.

Lizards have lots of enemies, including snakes. Lizards avoid being eaten by hiding and, if they are spotted, running away fast. Many lizards, if they are caught by the tail, can drop their tails and run off! The bones in their tails are cracked, and designed to drop off if twisted. The lizard will then grow a new tail.

The Australian frilled lizard raises its frill to scare its enemies.

Snakes are also hunted by other animals. They can often avoid capture by hiding and staying still. The rattlesnake warns off its enemies by shaking its tail, causing the loose scales at the end to rattle.

It's amazing!

The hognose snake pretends to be dead if it is disturbed!

Like pit vipers, rattlesnakes can sense the heat given off by nearby animals.

Babies

Some female lizards lay soft, leathery eggs in a hole in the ground. The eggs are warmed by the sun. Other lizards keep the eggs inside them until they are ready to hatch. This keeps the eggs warm and safe, but it slows the mother down. She, and the babies, are in more danger of being eaten. When they hatch the mother does not look after the babies. Baby lizards have to look after themselves.

An iguana lays up to 50 eggs at a time.

It's amazing!

Each baby shinglebacked lizard is more than half as long as its mother when it is born!

Like lizards, some snakes lay eggs, while others have live young that are small versions of the adult animal. A snake may lay up to 20 eggs at a time. Once she has laid the eggs, most female snakes leave them. They do not even wait until the eggs hatch.

Hognose snakes hatching

Fact file

Lizard

Largest
The komodo dragon can grow up to 3 m long and weigh over 160 kg.

Smallest
The virgin gorda gecko is only 36 mm long.

Oldest known
One male slow worm (a sort of lizard) lived for 54 years.

This komodo dragon is eating a goat.

Food
Most lizards eat insects. Big lizards eat meat. Komodo dragons eat animals as big as pigs and deer, and other dead animals. Some lizards just eat plants. The marine iguana eats seaweed.

Speed
The fastest lizard is the six-lined race-runner, which can run at 29 kph.

Snake

This reticulated python is swallowing a deer.

Longest
The reticulated python can reach between 6–10 m long!

Heaviest
The anaconda is almost twice as heavy as the reticulated python, weighing up to 227 kg.

Smallest
The thread snake measures only 108 mm long.

Oldest known
The longest lived snake was a common boa that lived for 40 years.

Food
Snakes eat meat – insects, frogs, lizards, fish and animals as big as a pig or a deer.

Speed
The fastest land snake is the black mamba. It can reach speeds of up to 19 kph.

Glossary

cold-blooded an animal that cannot heat up its own blood.

eardrums a thin piece of skin in the ear that helps animals hear.

glides moving through the air.

hibernate to sleep through the winter.

prey an animal that is hunted by another for food.

species a group of living things that are very similar.

reptiles snakes, lizards, crocodiles, turtles, tortoises and other animals that are cold-blooded and covered in scales.

scaly skin covered with thin hard plates for protection.

venom poison.

vibrations shaking movements.

vines plants that hang like ropes from trees.

Index